75 Blues Turnarounds

By Michael DoCampo with Toby Wine

T0088315

To access audio visit:
www.halleonard.com/mylibrary

Enter Code
7919-5598-9645-1689

Recording Credits:
Michael DoCampo, Guitar

Cover artwork by Levin Pfeufer

ISBN 978-1-57560-971-3

Visit Hal Leonard Online at
www.halleonard.com

Contents

Introduction

The blues exists not only as an independent idiom but also as an undeniable influence on nearly every other genre of contemporary music. Rock, pop, jazz, country, and even opera and modern orchestral styles have been informed by the sounds and sentiments of the blues. Countless practitioners, from amateur hobbyists to gigging professionals, pick up their guitars everyday and carry on the traditions of this vital, ever-evolving art form. The dedicated player must, by definition, be a restless one—not content to simply repeat past performances or mimic the artistry of their idols, but instead to seek out new ground while always advancing their understanding and command of this distinctive musical language. It is with this quest in mind that we present *75 Blues Turnarounds*, a collection of phrases designed to enhance the vocabulary of the blues guitarist.

About the Authors

Michael DoCampo

Michael DoCampo is a New York–based guitarist who has been working at his craft for more than 40 years. This journey has included rewarding experiences in recording, performing, and traveling, and it has allowed him to work with talents such as Nicky Hopkins, Mick Taylor, David Clayton-Thomas, and Freddie Paris. Mike currently performs locally and operates a project studio where he recorded two original, blues-based rock CDs, *Shades of Blue* and *Turns in the Road,* and produces music for others. "My style is American roots–based," says Mike, "and I draw from my collection of vintage guitars and amps for both color and inspiration." He was featured in John Stix's "Resume" column in the January 1993 edition of *Guitar for the Practicing Musician.*

Mike has had the pleasure of studying with outstanding teachers/players such as Arlen Roth, David Landau, Gilberto Pellerano, Kenn Chipkin, Richard Lieberson, and Tom Guarna. From 1989 to 1992, Mike and his partners, Ken and Kevin English, produced and moderated the instructional guitar show *Ten to Rock* on Staten Island Community Television. This was a great learning and teaching experience, as it involved presenting lessons in a concise way, utilizing a three-camera shoot and graphics. Over 60 half-hour shows were produced, which can still be seen on Staten Island Community Television. In 1991, the show was a winner of the National Federation of Local Cable Programmers' (now known as the Alliance for Community Media) Hometown USA Video Festival in Portland, Oregon.

As a left-handed player, Mike has had to deal with the issue of mentally inverting chord diagrams, which are written from a right-handed perspective. "This skill has given me great insights on how to help left-handed students deal with the image-perspective problem." Being left-handed is also an advantage for Mike when dealing with right-handed students: "When facing a right-handed student, the 'mirror image' allows for a quick read of where my hands are."

The audio was recorded at Champ Studio, where the engineer was Anthony Ungaro. The equipment used (left-handed where applicable) includes a 1958 Fender Stratocaster in Fiesta Red, a Fender Nocaster Reissue, a Gibson ES-335, a Gibson 1959 Les Paul, a 1987 Reissue Epiphone Joe Pass, Fender Jazz and Precision Basses, a 1953 Fender Tweed Deluxe amplifier, and a 1961 Fender Brownface Princeton amplifier.

Toby Wine

Toby Wine is a native New Yorker and a freelance guitarist, composer, arranger, and educator. He is a graduate of the Manhattan School of Music, where he studied composition with Manny Albam and Edward Green. Toby has performed with Philip Harper (of the Harper Brothers and Art Blakey's Jazz Messengers), Bob Mover, Ari Ambrose, Michael and Carolyn Leonhart (of Steely Dan), Peter Hartmann, Ian Hendrickson-Smith (of Sharon Jones and the Dap-Kings), Melee, Saycon (currently starring in *Fela!* on Broadway), Nakia Henry, and the Harlem-based rock band Kojomodibo Sun, among others. His arrangements and compositions can be heard on recordings by Tobias Gebb and Unit Seven (*Free at Last*), Phillip Harper (*Soulful Sin, The Thirteenth Moon*, Muse Records), Ari Ambrose (*Early Song*, Steeplechase), and Ian Hendrickson-Smith (*Up in Smoke*, Sharp Nine). Toby leads his own trio and septet, does studio sessions, and works as a sideman with a variety of tri-state–area bandleaders. He spent four years as the music librarian for the Carnegie Hall Jazz band and is currently an instructor at the Church Street School for Music and Art in Tribeca. He is the author of numerous Cherry Lane publications, including *1001 Blues Licks, The Art of Texas Blues, 150 Cool Jazz Licks in Tab, Steely Dan: Legendary Licks*, and *Cool Pedal Steel Licks for Guitar*.

A Few Notes on Common Basslines and Chord Progressions

The turnaround, the final two measures of the familiar 12-bar form, is perhaps the least understood harmonic component of the blues, particularly amongst beginner and intermediate players. Even those who have amassed a collection of pet phrases and licks to be played over this section often lack a full comprehension of both its harmonic implications and the immense possibilities the turnaround has to offer to the improvising guitarist. So, what exactly is happening here? Let's take a closer look at a few of the most commonly-used turnaround chord progressions in the blues.

I–I^6–IV–#iv°7–I$^6_4$–V7 with an Ascending Bass (1-3-4-#4-5-5)

This turnaround progression features an ascending line in which the bass rises to the major 3rd, 4th, and then #4th in measure 11 of the 12-bar form, with each note given a single beat. In the 12th measure, the line continues to rise to the 5th of the key, which is the bass note of two different chords that last for two beats each. In the key of C, this line would be C–E–F–F# in measure 11, continuing to end on G–G in measure 12. In the key of A the sequence would be A–C#–D–D#–E–E. This should be a familiar enough idea, but what is implied by this line? Essentially, the tonic chord (C) moves into an inversion (C/E) that leads to the IV chord (F), the #iv diminished 7th (F#°7), and then to the tonic in second inversion (C/G) before concluding on the V chord (G7), which turns us around to the top of a new 12-measure chorus. In the key of A this progression would be A–A/C#–D–D#°7–A/E–E7. Play through this sequence in a variety of keys to observe just how logically the progression moves from one step to the next.

I–I$^4_2$–IV^6–iv^6–I$^6_4$–V7 with a Descending Bass (1-♭7-6-♭6-5-5)

The next turnaround is equally common but descends instead. In C, the notes would be C–B♭–A–A♭ in measure 11, and then G–G in measure 12. Each of the first four chords gets one beat in 4/4, and the last two each get two beats. In the key of C, the progression is C–C7/B♭–F/A–Fm/A♭–C/G–G7, and in A the turnaround would be A–A7/G–D/F#–Dm/F–A/E–E7. Once again, play through these chords in a number of keys and get familiar with the inner workings of this extremely common progression.

Other Common Progressions

Many other turnaround sequences pop up throughout the various sub-genres of the blues. In the jazz style, the I–VI7–ii7–V7 progression is most common. In gospel-inspired blues, I–IV–I–V7 is often used, as is the variation I–IV–#iv°7–V7. Simpler turnarounds often move from just the I to the V, with each chord given an entire measure; the V may be preceded by a ♭VI7 chord. Chromatic moves show up less frequently, but progressions such as I–♭III7–II7–♭II7 can be heard in the more jazz-inspired blues tunes as well.

As you play through the 75 turnarounds in this book, take note of what is happening harmonically and what is being implied by the licks and phrases. Don't be content to simply pick up your axe and fly through the turnarounds—take an analytical stance and unearth the hidden chordal moves behind them. Even the most visceral and primitive blues styles have a logical harmonic structure at their core, and an in-depth examination will reveal unseen complexities that can affect your playing and understanding of the music profoundly.

 Note: Track 76 contains tuning pitches.

TRACK 76

Basic Turnarounds

These are essential turnaround licks in the keys of A and E that are useful additions to any guitarist's arsenal.

1 Descending Minor 3rds

This time-tested phrase is such a familiar part of the blues vocabulary that it should be learned in every key for easy access, regardless of the song or style.

TRACK 1

2 Descending Major 6ths

The wider interval leaps and string-skipping action of this lick makes it a little harder, but it's just as indispensible as the previous phrase.

TRACK 2

3 Combo Version of Turnarounds 1 and 2

The stretch in this jazzy turnaround can be a little difficult. Be sure to use your index finger for all 5th-fret notes.

TRACK 3

4 Ascending Movement with an E Pedal

This is another one with a difficult stretch. Use your index finger to barre the B and high E strings at the 5th fret while you ascend along the G string.

TRACK 4

5 In the Style of Robert Johnson

This one has an A pedal note on top and a descending line on the 4th string.

TRACK 5

6 Descending Movement with an A Pedal

The next lick mimics the action of the previous lick closely but adds another note to the chords, giving the phrase more of a jazz flavor than an old-school Delta blues vibe.

TRACK 6

7 Ascending and Descending Movement with an A Pedal

This is one of my favorites, and it's another one with a nice stretch. For a variation, play the notes of each chord individually while letting them ring.

TRACK 7

8 In the Style of Eric Clapton

This lick is similar to a turnaround Clapton used on "Key to the Highway." Here, the descending line is on the bottom rather than the top or inside of the chords.

TRACK 8

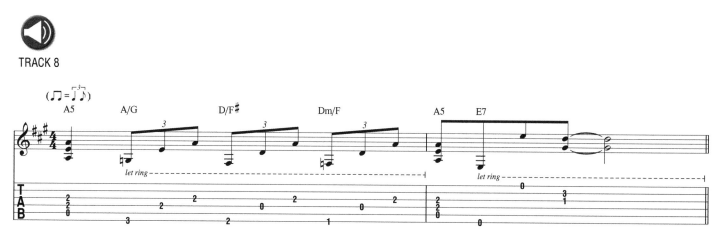

⑨ Descending Movement on Top

After the initial A power chord shape, use upstrokes to accentuate the descending melodic line played on the high E string.

TRACK 9

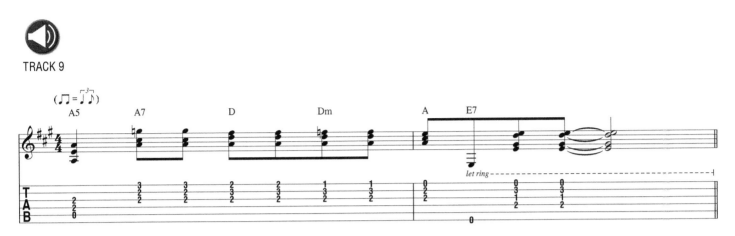

⑩ Jazzy Chord Voicings

Here, the turnaround is fleshed out into full chords. Check out the strongly melodic movement of the notes on each string, particularly the inside voices on the D and G strings.

TRACK 10

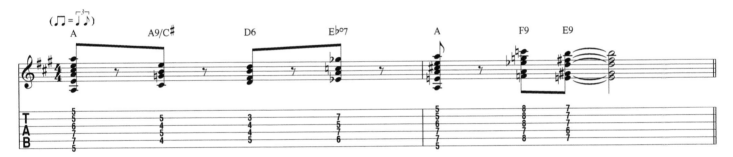

⑪ Ascending Movement with an A Pedal

Be sure to follow the "let ring" markings closely on this one. The A's on both the G and the open A strings should be allowed to ring throughout the first measure as the other voices ascend around them.

TRACK 11

12 Ascending Bass with an E Pedal

Note that the rest of the phrases in this chapter are in the key of E. This one pairs a rising line on the low E string with the droning B and high E strings above and requires precise fingerpicking to bring out its elegant character.

TRACK 12

13 Descending Major 6ths

This lick is very similar to an earlier phrase in A. The open strings in the second measure introduce a slight variation. This is meat and potatoes blues guitar—learn it in every key and position you can if you're serious about playing in this style!

TRACK 13

14 More Descending 6ths

Play this somewhat more intricate lick with your middle finger descending along the A string and your index finger taking the notes on the G string, including the trill that begins the second measure of the phrase.

TRACK 14

15 Descending 10ths

For this variation on the previous lick, play the wider 10th intervals with your middle finger on the low E string and your ring finger on the G string. The Beatles copped a bit of this traditional country blues flavor on their much-loved "Blackbird."

TRACK 15

16 In the Style of Jimmy Page

This one is reminiscent of Page's ascending turnaround in "Bring It on Home" from *Led Zeppelin II*. Use your index and middle fingers on the D and B strings, respectively, in the first measure.

TRACK 16

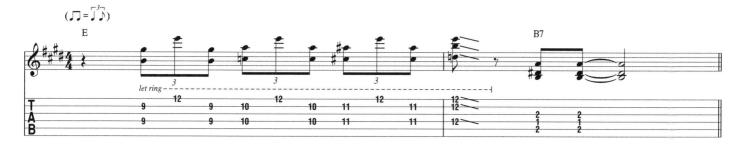

17 Tritone Turnaround

Try this one on for size. The bass player will need a heads-up to avoid clashing with the surprise A♯ in the first measure!

TRACK 17

Turnarounds in E

 **In the Style of Eric Clapton**

This is reminiscent of Clapton's work with John Mayall & the Bluesbreakers. Perform the bend, release, and pull-off on the G string with your middle finger.

TRACK 18

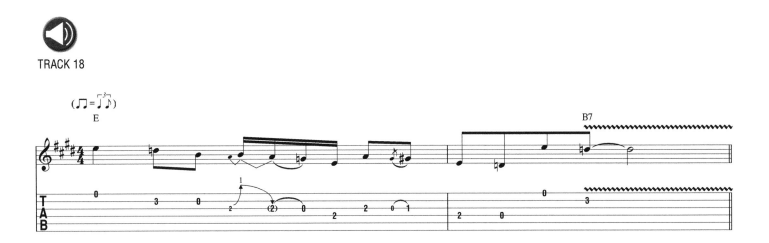

 **In the Style of Eric Clapton**

This one brings to mind a turnaround Clapton played in John Mayall & the Bluesbreakers' version of "Hide Away." Note the "pitch-matching" technique in measure 2, where the open high E string is followed by another E on the B string—a favorite device of blues guitarists going all the way back to the original Delta practitioners.

TRACK 19

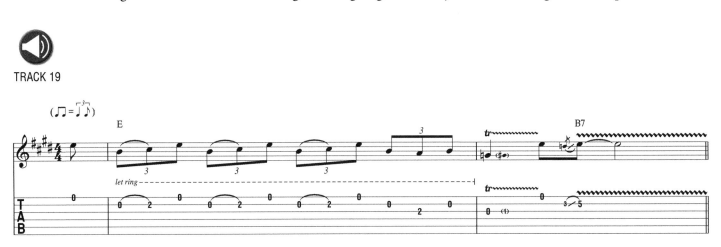

20 In the Style of Stevie Ray Vaughan

The double stops and minor 3rds (G) over the tonic chord (E) give this one some rough-edged Texas blues flavor.

TRACK 20

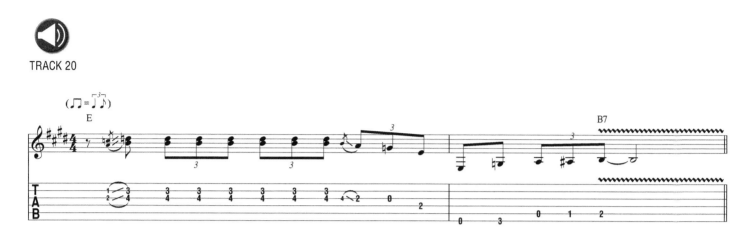

21 In the Style of Stevie Ray Vaughan with a Nod to Johnny Winter

This lick includes both the minor 3rd (G) and the ♭5th (B♭). Low-register playing like this has traditionally been a favorite of Winter's and his late, great musical descendant, Stevie Ray.

TRACK 21

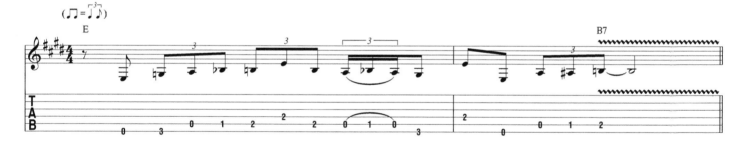

Turnarounds in A

 In the Style of Eric Clapton

This turnaround for an A blues is similar to one that Clapton uses in "Crossroads."

TRACK 22

23 **In the Style of Eric Clapton**

Here's another one that's reminiscent of Clapton's work with John Mayall & the Bluesbreakers. The high register demands extra precision from the fretting hand, thanks to the extremely close quarters.

TRACK 23

24 In the Style of Eric Clapton

Here's just one more in the style of Slow Hand's work with John Mayall & the Bluesbreakers. Stay in 5th position throughout the phrase, but use your ring finger for the 8th-fret quarter step bends, Clapton-style.

TRACK 24

25 In the Style of B.B. King

The great B.B. is fond of the major pentatonic scale (A–B–C#–E–F# in the key of A) and uses its characteristic major 3rd and 6th tones liberally, often bending the 5th to the 6th and back as in the lick that follows.

TRACK 25

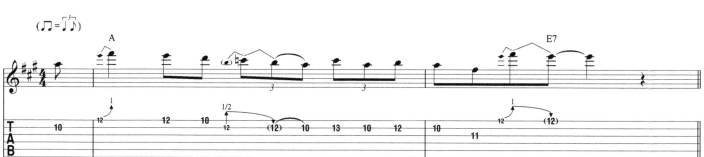

26 In the Style of B.B. King

B.B. also uses repetition to great effect. The repeated chromatic triplets in the first measure below are right out of his book. Be sure to use your middle finger for the slide up the B string in the second measure, putting yourself in good position to finish out the phrase.

TRACK 26

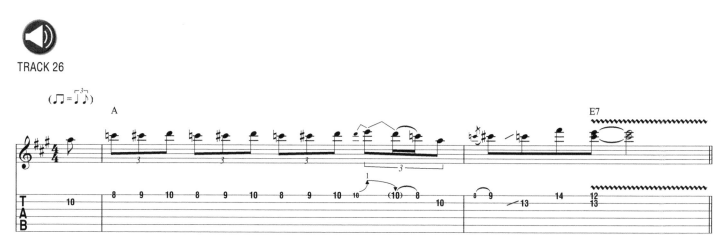

Turnarounds in C

27 Double Stops in the Style of Chuck Berry

Berry was a whiz with double-stop phrases, using them to bridge the gaps between jazz, blues, and early rock 'n' roll. This phrase is typical of his most influential work.

TRACK 27

28 Double Stops in the Style of Chuck Berry

Here's a somewhat more intricate variation on the previous phrase. Try transposing this one to various keys and areas of the neck so you can use these sweet-sounding double stops whenever the mood strikes you, regardless of the key or context!

TRACK 28

29 In the Style of T-Bone Walker

The composer of "Stormy Monday" was the original virtuoso of electric blues guitar; he paved the way for generations of guitar slingers to follow. Equally adept at single-note, double-stop, and melodic chord-style playing, T-Bone had a knack for combining them all and marrying the blues to jazz as in the soulful phrase below.

TRACK 29

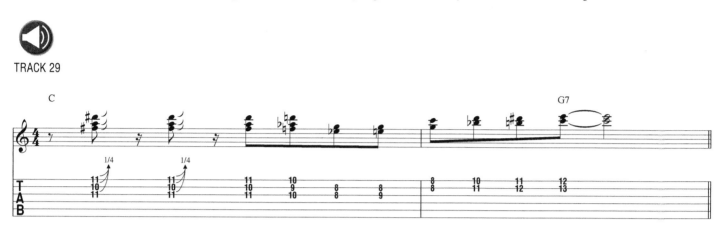

30 In the Style of T-Bone Walker

Here's another turnaround in the spirit of this enormously influential bluesman. Note the use of both chromatic approach notes (the D♯–F♯ double stop that opens the phrase) and major and minor 3rds over the C chord (D♯ and E).

TRACK 30

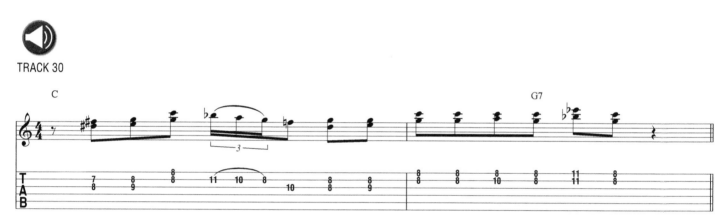

31 More Double Stops in C

The old-school double stops in this phrase bring to mind the work of the honky-tonk pianists whose work pre-dated the rise of the virtuoso single-note guitar soloists of the 1960s. Phrases like these are timeless, however, and still sound right at home in a modern blues context.

TRACK 31

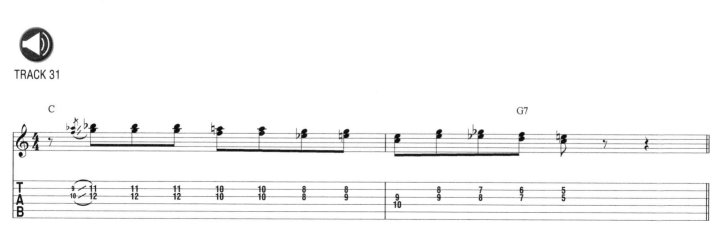

Turnarounds in G

32 In the Style of Mike Bloomfield

The trills and bends of this 3rd-position, G minor pentatonic phrase are now stock material in every blues guitarist's arsenal. All of the bends should be performed by the ring finger, with the middle and index fingers lined up behind it on the string to aid in the push.

TRACK 32

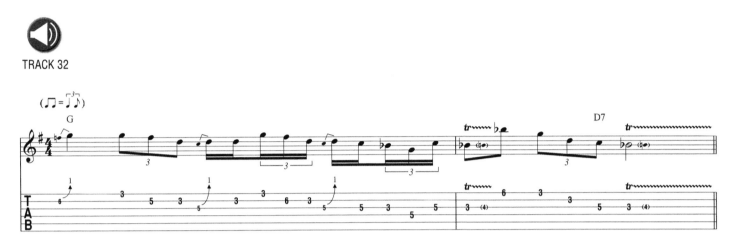

33 In the Style of Clapton . . . with a Stutter

Here's another one reminiscent of Clapton's work with John Mayall & the Bluesbreakers. Take a look at that "stutter" move, courtesy of a carefully placed rest and the somewhat more complex, broken triplet rhythms.

TRACK 33

34 Reminiscent of "Strange Brew"

Add some tubular fuzz to your tone and dig into this lick that captures a little of Cream's funky, psychedelic '60s vibe.

TRACK 34

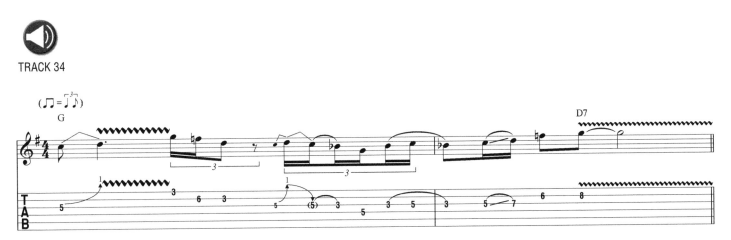

35 In the Style of B.B. King with a Robben Ford Ending

The major pentatonic moves here, which emphasize the 6th of the chord (E), are pure B.B., while the register jump and countrified 15th-fret bend give a nod to modern blues and fusion master Ford.

TRACK 35

36 In the Style of Albert Collins with a Johnny Winter Tag

Winter and the late, telecaster-slinging Collins shared a Texas heritage and a penchant for slashing, hard-driving blues guitar. The downward rake in measure 1 is reminiscent of Collins' angular soloing, while Winter often performs wide leaps across strings such as those found in measure 2.

TRACK 36

Jazzy Blues Turnarounds in B♭

Note that the turnarounds in this chapter are played over a I7–VI7–ii7–V7 chord progression, the most common turnaround employed in a jazz-style blues. In B♭, the chords are B♭7–G7–Cm7–F7. The second and fourth chords are commonly altered to include a ♭9th or ♯9th.

37 In the Style of T-Bone Walker and Charlie Christian

These are two of the most important and influential guitarists to ever pick up the instrument, and if you're at all unfamiliar with their work, you owe it to yourself to rectify that situation. Friends and contemporaries, the two men were the first electric soloists of note and accomplishment. Walker moved in the blues and R&B realm, while Christian plied his trade in the jazz world, and most notably as a member of Benny Goodman's outfit—the first major group to combine both black and white musicians. Walker and Christian broke away from the often heavy-handed rhythm guitar styles of their era and soared during single-note solos in the spirit of the great saxophone and trumpet players of the day. Amplification provided the long sought-after volume they needed to be heard over a band.

TRACK 37

38 In the Style of T-Bone Walker and Charlie Christian

The smooth eighth note lines and staccato quarter notes below are emblematic of the era when swing began to move towards the more complex bebop style created by saxophonist Charlie Parker ("Bird"), trumpeter Dizzy Gillespie, and pianist Bud Powell. Christian bridged the gap between these jazz styles beautifully and found himself equally at home with both of the often-contentious factions standing on either side of the stylistic divide.

TRACK 38

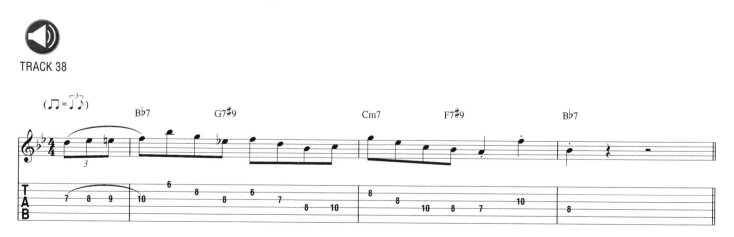

39 In the Style of T-Bone Walker and Charlie Christian

Jazz players sprinkle their lines liberally with chromatic "approach" notes, such as the C♯ and the F♯ in the phrase that follows. Each note approaches a chord tone from a half step (one fret) below. This can be a colorful and exciting device, even if you're a blues or rock purist.

TRACK 39

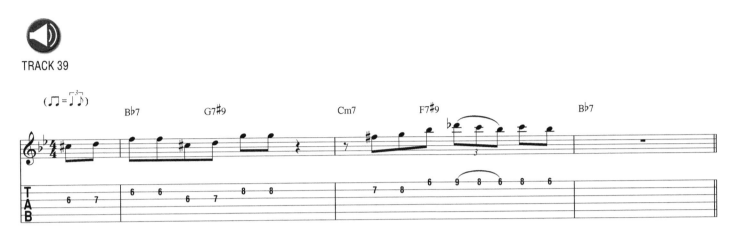

40 Jazzy Double Stops

Use your first finger to barre at the 3rd fret and then at the 6th fret when you switch positions at the end of the first measure. This one really brings the worlds of jazz and blues together!

TRACK 40

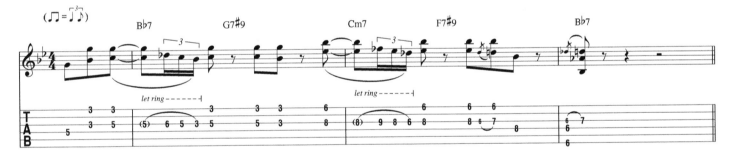

41 Flat 3rds and 13ths

Here's a classic jazz phrase that clearly illustrates the concepts of arpeggio-based playing, in which the individual chords are outlined, and the use of chromatic-approach (F♯–G) and "connector" notes, as in the C–C♯–D of the second measure.

TRACK 41

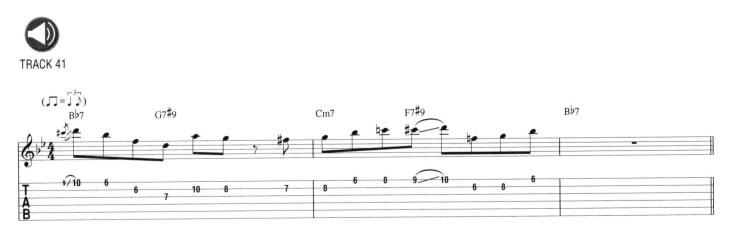

Gospel Blues Turnarounds in C

Each turnaround in this chapter follows a I–I7–IV–#iv°7–I progression (in C, C–C7–F–F#°7–C), a favorite of gospel practitioners and the blues stylists they have influenced.

42 C Blues with a Double-Stop Slide

This phrase shifts positions three times, rising from 5th position in the first measure to 8th and 11th positions in measure 2. Use your ring finger for the B-string slides to both the 10th and 13th frets.

TRACK 42

43 C Blues with Major and Minor 3rds

All blues styles play with the contrast and combination of major and minor sounds—an idea central to the genre both musically and philosophically. The phrase below neatly demonstrates this duality by juxtaposing both E and E♭ in each measure in a way that's both typical and beautiful. If all you're doing is playing the minor pentatonic scale, you're missing a world of choices, sounds, and possibilities!

TRACK 43

44 In the Style of Eric Clapton

This turnaround is reminiscent of EC's work with Derek and the Dominos. Perform each bend with the ring finger.

TRACK 44

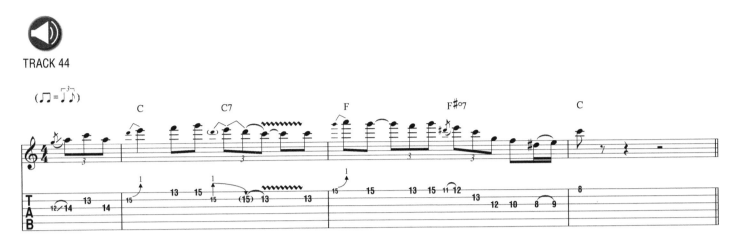

45 In the Style of Eric Clapton, Albert Collins, and Roy Buchanan

This next turnaround is a hybrid of the styles of all three guitarists. Be sure to pull the A-string bend towards the floor—a typical Buchanan move.

TRACK 45

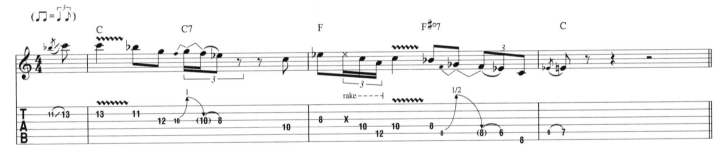

46 Gospel C Blues with a Pre-Bend

Here, the B string must be bent up a half step from G to A♭ *before* you strike it. Play the A♭ at the 9th fret first to hear your target pitch. Pre-bending is a difficult technique to master and requires both a good ear for intonation and an intimate knowledge of your instrument, as every guitar is slightly different in terms of the finger strength required to push a string up to a desired pitch with an acceptable degree of accuracy. Be patient!

TRACK 46

Driving Rhythm Turnarounds in A

 47 **In the Style of Johnny Winter**

Here, the simplified harmonic progression (I–V) leaves ample space for this blues scale–based low-register riff in the style of the Texas master.

TRACK 47

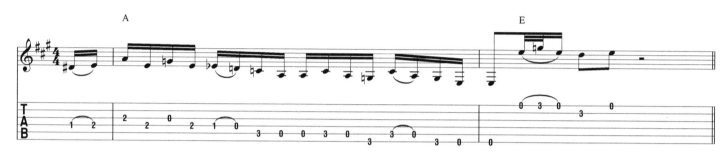

 48 **Country/Rock Style**

You'll need to use a hybrid picking style (pick and fingers) for this one. A heavy Telecaster tone is recommended—this is working man's blues on steroids! Stay in 5th position throughout the phrase.

TRACK 48

49 In the Style of Procol Harum

This blues/rock turnaround is similar to a lick Robin Trower plays on "Whiskey Train." Use your middle finger for the slide up the G string in the second measure, as this will put you in good position to perform those sliding 6ths with your ring finger on the high E string.

TRACK 49

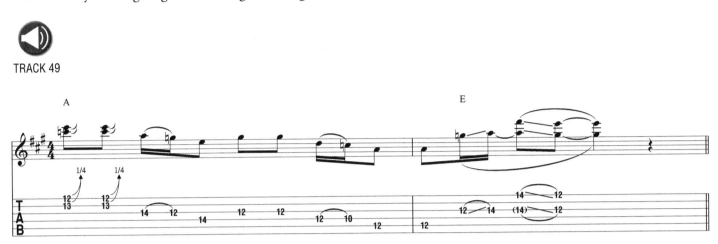

50 In the Style of Clapton plus ZZ Top

This blues/rock turnaround has a kind of Clapton/ZZ Top/Reverend Billy C. Wirtz vibe. It's a fairly simple A minor pentatonic lick played in 8th position.

TRACK 50

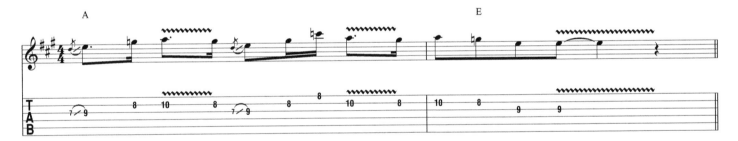

51 In the Style of Jeff Beck

This is reminiscent of Beck's early work. The pull-offs in the first measure hint at the wealth of ideas that are possible when adding open strings to licks played in higher positions.

TRACK 51

An Assortment of Turnarounds in the Style of Guitar Masters

🄓🄔 In the Style of Mike Bloomfield and Wayne Bennett

Here's a classic blues scale–based turnaround inspired by Bloomfield and the criminally underrated Bennett, best known for his work with the soulful vocalist Bobby "Blue" Bland.

🔊

TRACK 52

🄓🄔 In the Style of Jimmie Vaughan plus Clapton

This intricate little phrase features the finely detailed moves and position shifts favored by both Clapton and the always-tasteful Vaughan, the older brother of the late Stevie Ray. If you're still stuck in the blues box of one-position pentatonic playing, this turnaround will help you break free and get you moving up and down the neck.

🔊

TRACK 53

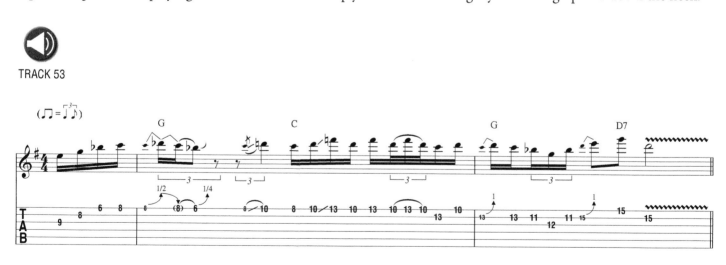

54 In the Style of Mike Bloomfield

The great Chicago guitarist loved ornate turnaround phrases like the one below, full of quarter step bends and broken triplet rhythms. It's a prime example of just how much can be achieved while staying *in* the aforementioned blues box!

TRACK 54

55 In the Style of the Allman Brothers

This one has a little bit of Dickey Betts and little bit of Duane Allman. Begin with a middle-finger slide up the G string, bend the high E string with your ring finger, and then drop down to 3rd position to finish out the phrase with classic G blues scale ideas.

TRACK 55

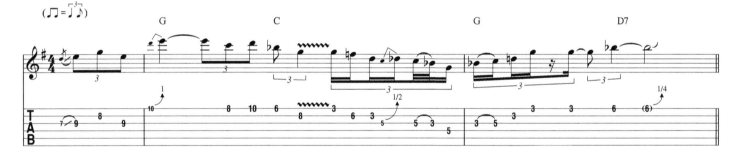

56 In the Style of Duane Allman

This one has a little bit of DoCampo in it, too. Slides facilitate positional shifts, while the notes are a combination of both major and minor pentatonic scales in G.

TRACK 56

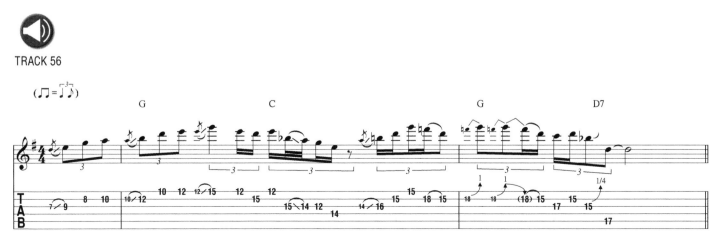

Turnarounds in C#

57 **In the Style of Albert King**

Don't use a pick for this one if you want to replicate the sound of the King, who decided on a thumb-picking style after discovering his penchant for dropping the plectrum.

TRACK 57

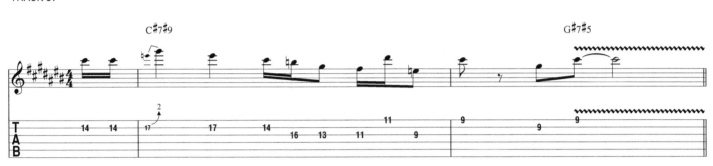

59 **In the Style of Albert King**

Try fingerpicking this classic turnaround phrase as well. The pure, minor pentatonic sound is augmented by the addition of the major 3rd (E#) in the second measure.

TRACK 58

59 In the Style of Jimi Hendrix and Robin Trower

This one combines the electrifying styles of both Hendrix and the popular Procol Harum axe man. The C♯ minor pentatonic scale is employed in a 4th-position fingering for the majority of the lick.

TRACK 59

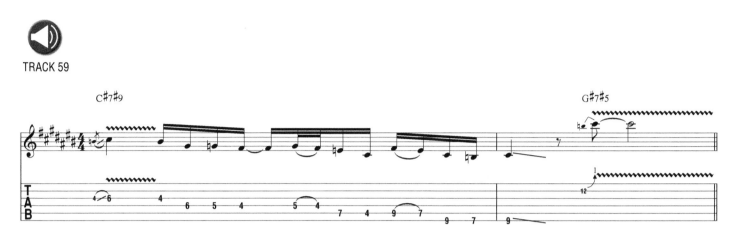

60 More of that Jimi-Robin Thang

This turnaround finds us back in the more familiar 9th-position C♯ minor pentatonic fingering and includes some truly classic bending moves.

TRACK 60

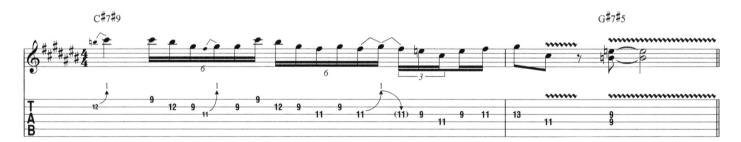

More Turnarounds in E

61 In the Style of Jimmy Page

This turnaround begins with a unison bend in which the E on the high E string, played by the index finger, is matched by the ring finger bending the B string up a whole step at the 15th fret.

TRACK 61

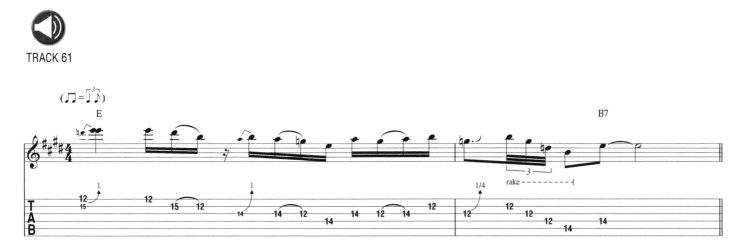

62 Open-String Turnaround

This one downshifts twice, from its beginning in 7th position to the drop to 4th position, and finally into an open-string configuration. Note the use of both major 3rds (G#) and 6ths (C#).

TRACK 62

63 Double-Stop Bends

The slide in the second measure should be performed by the middle finger, with the index finger taking the 7th-fret, high E-string notes that follow.

TRACK 63

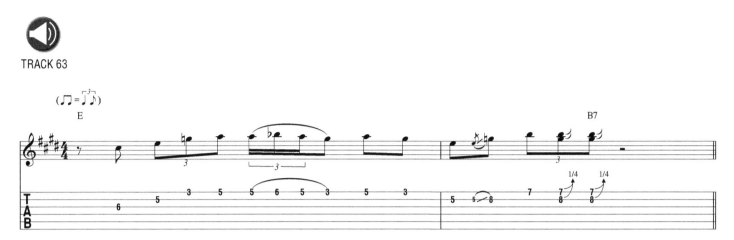

64 Major Pentatonic Turnaround

The sunnier sound of the major pentatonic scale provides a nice contrast to the more commonplace minor pentatonic licks. Both the downwards slide and the subsequent bend on the G string should be played by the ring finger.

TRACK 64

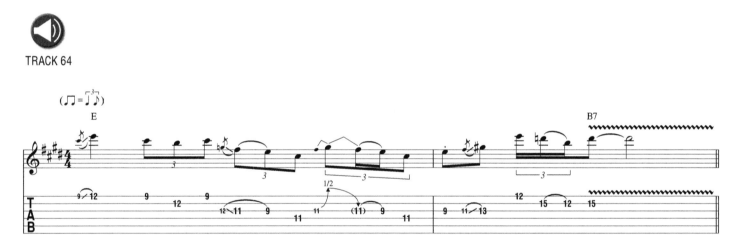

65 Repeated Bends

Here's a simple turnaround lick that gets its punch from the vocal cry of the repeated high E-string bends in the first measure. The final bend really soars into the stratosphere.

TRACK 65

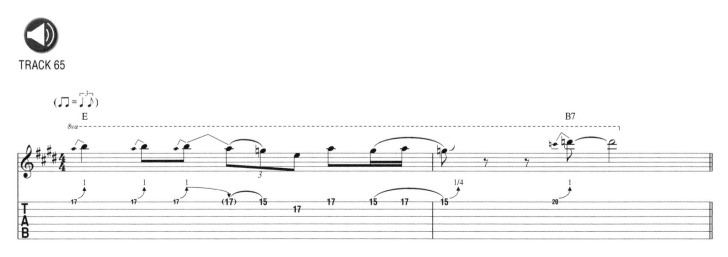

More Turnarounds in C

66 Double-Stop Turnaround

Repetition is an oft-ignored improvisatory tool. The repeated triplet double stops in the turnaround below will push the rhythm section along with you and raise the excitement level noticeably.

TRACK 66

67 Pivoting Triplets

After the initial B-string bend, the descending triplets pivot between A and B♭ as they are pulled off to the G below and followed by the D♯ on the B string.

TRACK 67

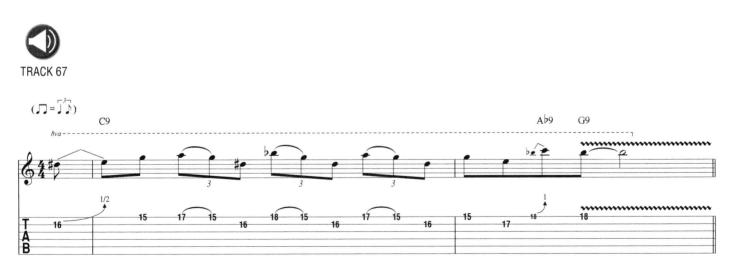

68 Pentatonic Triplets

This is real meat-and-potatoes stuff—classic minor pentatonic box playing (save for the D note on the high E string) from the heart of the blues guitar vocabulary.

TRACK 68

69 High-Register Turnaround

This turnaround in the higher regions of the neck nicely outlines the C minor pentatonic scale in a 15th-position fingering. Play the final 20th-fret bend with your ring finger and follow with your pinky on the high E string.

TRACK 69

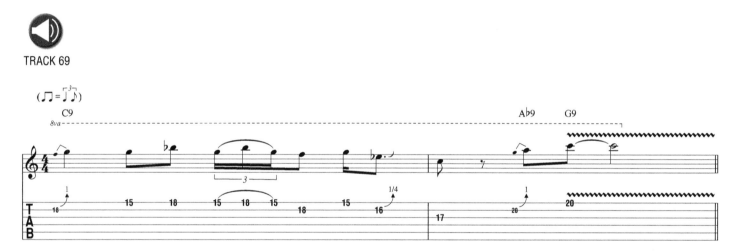

70 In the Style of Jimmie Vaughan and Eric Clapton

Start this one with the index finger both bending the high E string and sliding down the B string into the 8th-position C minor pentatonic fingering.

TRACK 70

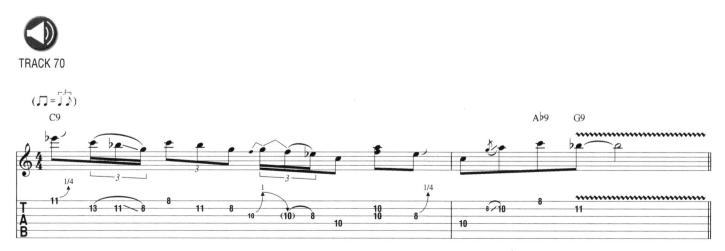

Assorted Turnarounds in B Minor by the Three Kings

71 In the Style of B.B. King

This turnaround stays strictly in 7th position. Use your ring finger for the high E-string bend in measure 1 and for the G-string bend-and-release in measure 2.

TRACK 71

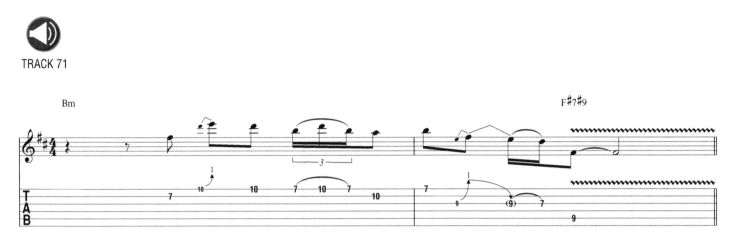

72 In the Style of the Three Kings

This phrase is one part Albert, one part B.B., and one part Freddie—in every way, classic minor blues vocabulary.

TRACK 72

73 Percussive Punch and Vibrato

This one really speaks with its variety of articulation techniques, from the downwards slide that begins the phrase to the subtle bends and singing vibrato used in each measure.

TRACK 73

74 In the Style of Albert King

Here, you're playing "in the cracks" of pitch and time. Push that bend up a whole step accurately, and then let it gently come down a half step to E♭. Tasty stuff!

TRACK 74

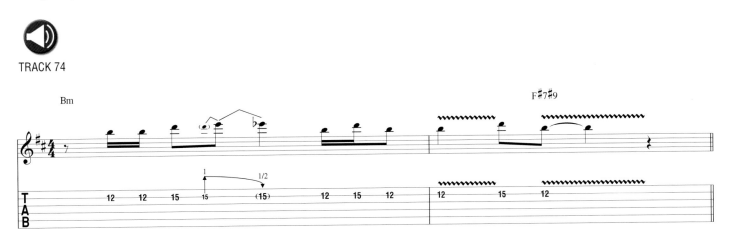

75 In the Style of Freddie King

This lick is a truly fitting way to end our exploration of the turnaround. It's simple, soulful, and direct—the way the blues should be. Virtuoso technique and a ton of notes can never take the place of good, honest, and emotional playing in this style. Enjoy!

TRACK 75

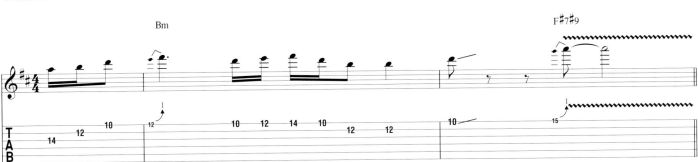

GUITAR NOTATION LEGEND

Guitar music can be notated three different ways: on a *musical staff*, in *tablature*, and in *rhythm slashes*.

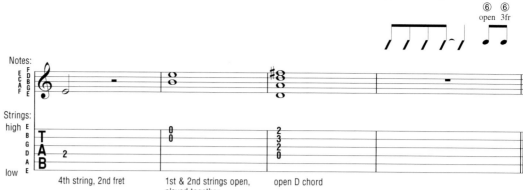

RHYTHM SLASHES are written above the staff. Strum chords in the rhythm indicated. Use the chord diagrams found at the top of the first page of the transcription for the appropriate chord voicings. Round noteheads indicate single notes.

THE MUSICAL STAFF shows pitches and rhythms and is divided by bar lines into measures. Pitches are named after the first seven letters of the alphabet.

TABLATURE graphically represents the guitar fingerboard. Each horizontal line represents a string, and each number represents a fret.

4th string, 2nd fret   1st & 2nd strings open, played together   open D chord

---

HALF-STEP BEND: Strike the note and bend up 1/2 step.

WHOLE-STEP BEND: Strike the note and bend up one step.

GRACE NOTE BEND: Strike the note and immediately bend up as indicated.

SLIGHT (MICROTONE) BEND: Strike the note and bend up 1/4 step.

BEND AND RELEASE: Strike the note and bend up as indicated, then release back to the original note. Only the first note is struck.

PRE-BEND: Bend the note as indicated, then strike it.

VIBRATO: The string is vibrated by rapidly bending and releasing the note with the fretting hand.

WIDE VIBRATO: The pitch is varied to a greater degree by vibrating with the fretting hand.

HAMMER-ON: Strike the first (lower) note with one finger, then sound the higher note (on the same string) with another finger by fretting it without picking.

PULL-OFF: Place both fingers on the notes to be sounded. Strike the first note and without picking, pull the finger off to sound the second (lower) note.

LEGATO SLIDE: Strike the first note and then slide the same fret-hand finger up or down to the second note. The second note is not struck.

SHIFT SLIDE: Same as legato slide, except the second note is struck.

TRILL: Very rapidly alternate between the notes indicated by continuously hammering on and pulling off.

TAPPING: Hammer ("tap") the fret indicated with the pick-hand index or middle finger and pull off to the note fretted by the fret hand.

NATURAL HARMONIC: Strike the note while the fret-hand lightly touches the string directly over the fret indicated.

PINCH HARMONIC: The note is fretted normally and a harmonic is produced by adding the edge of the thumb or the tip of the index finger of the pick hand to the normal pick attack.

PICK SCRAPE: The edge of the pick is rubbed down (or up) the string, producing a scratchy sound.

MUFFLED STRINGS: A percussive sound is produced by laying the fret hand across the string(s) without depressing, and striking them with the pick hand.

PALM MUTING: The note is partially muted by the pick hand lightly touching the string(s) just before the bridge.

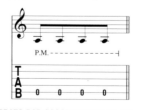

RAKE: Drag the pick across the strings indicated with a single motion.

TREMOLO PICKING: The note is picked as rapidly and continuously as possible.

VIBRATO BAR DIVE AND RETURN: The pitch of the note or chord is dropped a specified number of steps (in rhythm), then returned to the original pitch.

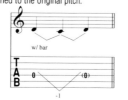

VIBRATO BAR SCOOP: Depress the bar just before striking the note, then quickly release the bar.

VIBRATO BAR DIP: Strike the note and then immediately drop a specified number of steps, then release back to the original pitch.